Ilka List

Moths and Butterflies
of North America

Franklin Watts - A Division of Scholastic Inc.
New York • Toronto • London • Auckland • Sydney
Mexico City • New Delhi • Hong Kong
Danbury, Connecticut

6/02

For Rose, Isabella, and Alexandra,
fair as the breeze dancing with butterflies

Photographs ©: BBC Natural History Unit: 5 bottom fight (Jose B. Ruiz), 5 top left, 35 (Lynn Stone), 5 top right (Doug Weclisler); Dembinsky Photo Assoc.: 19 (Sharon Cummings), 29 (E.R. Degginger), 24, 25 (John Gerlach), 7 (Gary Meszaros), 17, 31, 37 (Skip Moody), 5 bottom left (Rod Planck), 1 (Ted & Jean Reuther); Peter Arnold Inc./Hans Pfletschinger: 33; Photo Researchers, NY: 41 (Charles V. Angelo), 6, 12, 13 (Danny Brass), 21 (Michael P. Gadomski); Visuals Unlimited: 43 (Robert Clay), 15 (Robert W. Domm), 23 (Joe McDonald), 42 (Kjell B. Sandved), cover (John Serra), 27, 39 (Leroy Simon).

Illustrations by Pedro Julio Gonzalez, Steve Savage and A. Natacha Pimentel C.

The photo on the cover shows a cabbage white butterfly. The photo on the title page shows a cecropia moth emerging from its cocoon.

Library of Congress Cataloging-in-Publication Data

List, Ilka
   Moths and butterflies of North America / Ilka List; [Pedro Julio Gonzalez,
Steve Savage, and A. Natacha Pimentel C., illustrators].
      p. cm. — (Animals in order)
      Includes bibliographical references and index.
      ISBN 0-531-11597-6
      1. Lepidoptera—North America—Juvenile literature. [1. Moths. 2. Butterflies.]
      I. Gonzalez, Pedro Julio, ill. II. Savage, Steve, 1965-ill. III. Titles. IV. Series.

QL548.L57 2001
595.78'097—dc21

                                                                    2001017960

GROLIER
PUBLISHING

Contents

A Look at Moths and Butterflies

Have you ever felt the soft wings of a fluttering moth brush against your cheek at night? Have you ever seen a small white butterfly dash out of the deep grass in a sunny field?

Although you would have seen one of these *insects* at night and the other during the day, there are ways in which they are similar. Scientists place moths and butterflies in the same *order,* or group, of animals. They have some traits in common that other animals don't share. The photographs on the next page show two moths and two butterflies. Can you see how they are similar?

Cecropia moth

Luna moth

Mourning cloak butterfly

Monarch butterfly

Traits of Moths and Butterflies

Moths and butterflies are all members of an order of insects called lepidoptera (lep-ih-DOP-ter-a). This scientific name means "scaly wings." The overlapping *scales* on their wings can be very colorful. When you touch the wings of a butterfly or moth, the delicate scales fall off like powder.

Butterfly wings are often large, rounded, and brightly colored. In flight, the front and hind wings move together as one wing. Resting butterflies hold their wings up vertically over their backs so the wing tops are together and the undersides show.

Many moths have long, slender wings. The front and hind wings latch together with delicate thread-like strands called filaments. Moths fold their wings down rooflike over their backs or open them out flat.

Moths and butterflies have long, tubelike mouths that they use to suck liquids. They feed only on fluids, and most prefer to feed on flower juices. They may also drink the mineral-filled fluid found in puddles and animal droppings.

Can you see this moth's long, tubelike mouth?

Some adult moths never eat at all. They live on stored fat.

Most butterflies fly during the day while moths are sleeping. Most moths prefer to fly in the dark. Butterflies and moths have large, compound eyes.

Moths and butterflies have *antennae* with which they sense the world. Butterfly antennae are long and thin with tiny clubs at their tips, while moth antennae are usually feathery and have no clubs.

When adult moths and butterflies lay eggs, they attach them to food that the hatching *larvae* will like. Baby caterpillars eat until they are too fat for their own *exoskeletons*. Then they split out of their small

Luna moths have feathery antennae.

exoskeletons and form bigger ones. Caterpillars go through several stages of growth. In the *pupa* stage, a moth caterpillar makes a *cocoon* and then changes into an adult. A butterfly caterpillar makes a *chrysalis*. In the pupa stage, the caterpillar undergoes a complete *metamorphosis*. It changes into a moth or a butterfly. Then it breaks out of the pupa, pumps up its wings, and flies.

The Order of Living Things

A tiger has more in common with a house cat than with a daisy. A true bug is more like a butterfly than a jellyfish. Scientists arrange living things into groups based on how they look and how they act. A tiger and a house cat belong to the same group, but a daisy belongs to a different group.

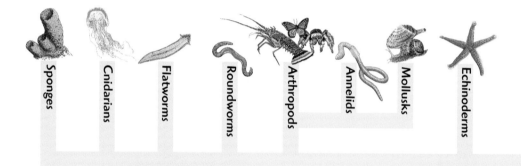

Sponges | Cnidarians | Flatworms | Roundworms | Arthropods | Annelids | Mollusks | Echinoderms

Plants | Fungi | Animals

Monerans | Protists

All living things can be placed in one of five groups called *kingdoms:* the plant kingdom, the animal kingdom, the fungus kingdom, the moneran kingdom, and the protist kingdom. You can probably name many of the creatures in the plant or animal kingdoms. The fungus kingdom includes mushrooms, yeasts, and molds. The moneran and protist kingdoms contain thousands of living things that are too small to see without a microscope.

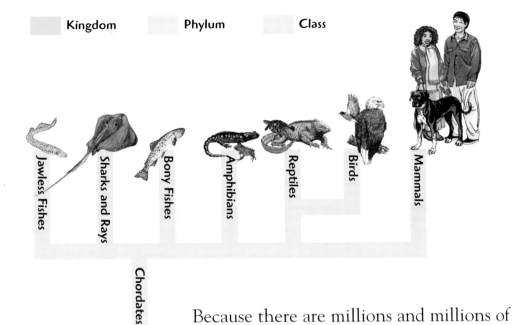

Kingdom   Phylum   Class

Jawless Fishes · Sharks and Rays · Bony Fishes · Amphibians · Reptiles · Birds · Mammals

Chordates

Because there are millions and millions of living things on Earth, some of the members of one kingdom may not seem all that similar. The animal kingdom includes creatures as different as tarantulas and trout, jellyfish and jaguars, salamanders and sparrows, elephants and earthworms.

To show that an elephant is more like a jaguar than an earthworm, scientists further separate the creatures in each kingdom into more specific groups. The animal kingdom can be divided into nine *phyla.* Humans belong to the chordate phylum. All chordates have a backbone.

Each phylum can be subdivided into many *classes.* Humans, mice, and elephants all belong to the mammal class. Each class can be further subdivided into orders, orders into *families,* families into *genera,* and genera into *species.* All the members of a species are very similar.

How Moths and Butterflies Fit In

You can probably guess that moths and butterflies belong to the animal kingdom. They have much more in common with spiders and snakes than with maple trees and morning glories.

Moths and butterflies belong to the arthropod phylum. All arthropods have a hard, shiny outer coat. Can you guess what other living things might be arthropods? Examples include spiders, scorpions, mites, ticks, millipedes, and centipedes. Some arthropods live in the ocean. Lobsters, crabs, and shrimps all belong to this group.

The arthropod phylum can be divided into a number of classes. Moths and butterflies belong to the insect class. Bugs, ants, flies, and beetles are also insects.

There are thirty different orders of insects. The lepidopterans make up one of these orders. Lepidopterans can be divided into a number of different families and genera. These groups can be broken down into thousands of species. They live in many different kinds of *habitats*—valleys, mountains, deserts, and even the Arctic Circle. In this book, you will learn more about fifteen species of moths and butterflies that live in North America.

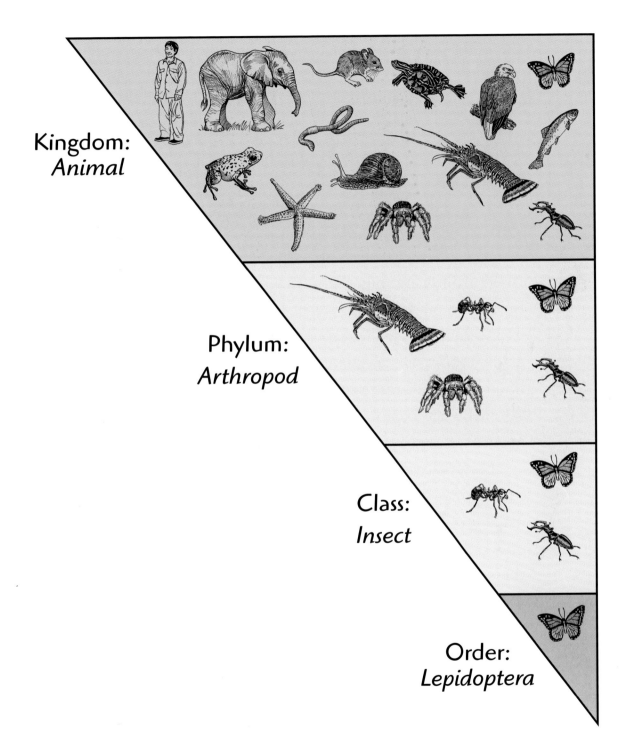

Kingdom:
Animal

Phylum:
Arthropod

Class:
Insect

Order:
Lepidoptera

11

Whites and Sulphurs

FAMILY: Pieridae
COMMON EXAMPLE: Cabbage white butterfly
GENUS AND SPECIES: *Pieris rapae*
WINGSPAN: 1 1/4 to 2 7/8 inches (33 to 72 mm)

Insect stowaways sometimes travel long distances hidden on plants. Perhaps that is how cabbage whites came to Canada from Europe and Asia in about 1860. Now they live all across North America. When you wander through a field in summer, visit a garden, or explore a city park, you may stir up some cabbage white butterflies.

Both male and female cabbage whites have white wings with black tips. Females have two black spots on their forewings, while males have only one. When cabbage whites rest, they hold their wings up vertically over their backs. Then their yellowish undersides show.

Female cabbage whites usually lay their eggs on popular garden plants, such as cabbage, radishes, and broccoli. These plants have special oils, called mustard oils, in their leaves. A female can choose the right plant food for her young by tasting the oils in the leaves with her feet.

At first an egg is creamy white, but it turns orange when it is ready to hatch. A female cabbage white avoids laying a new egg near an orange egg. She lays it on a separate leaf so her young won't have to share their food. The new baby caterpillars are downy and green with yellowish stripes.

Swallowtails and Parnassians

FAMILY: Papilionidae
COMMON EXAMPLE: Black swallowtail
GENUS AND SPECIES: *Papilio polyxenes*
WINGSPAN: 2 5/8 to 3 1/2 inches (66 to 88 mm)

A black swallowtail butterfly drifts across a garden. It stops, drifts, stops, and drifts. It flies gracefully and lazily, but just try to catch it! This butterfly takes off in a straight line and gets away easily.

Swallowtails have black bodies and blue-black wings with yellow or orange dots in colorful bands along the edges. There is usually a large yellow or orange spot on the inner edge of the hind wings. Each hind wing has something that looks like a little tail. The males and females look almost the same and are similar in size, but the female has a brighter band of blue spots on her hind wing.

If you are in a garden, you may see a swallowtail dip down, touch some vegetable leaves, and lay its round yellow eggs. Look closely for them on deep green parsley or carrot leaves.

When swallowtail eggs hatch, the baby caterpillars are black and white. They look much like bird droppings. As they eat, *molt*, and grow older, they turn bright green with black stripes and yellow dots. These new colors match the plants they eat. Each of these caterpillars has a gland that can poke up from behind its head. The gland is forked and produces a smell that drives enemies away.

Milkweed Butterflies

FAMILY: Danaidae
COMMON EXAMPLE: Monarch butterfly
GENUS AND SPECIES: *Danaus plexippus*
WINGSPAN: 3 1/2 to 4 inches (88 to 101 mm)

In late summer or fall, monarch butterflies are a common sight in flower gardens and city parks. Their colorful wings warn birds and mice, "Don't eat me! I'll make you sick!" Their black bodies contain poisons from the milkweed plants on which the caterpillars dined. They also store fat that will give them energy when they *migrate* south.

Short days and temperatures below 59 degrees Fahrenheit (15 degrees Celsius) signal monarchs to start their long journey south. They must leave the North before they freeze. East of the Rocky Mountains, most monarchs fly about 3,000 miles (4,828 km) to Mexico. West of the Rockies, monarchs fly to several places along the California coast. Hang gliders and balloonists have seen monarchs riding air currents as high as 7,000 feet (2,134 m). At times, monarchs speed along on the winds of hurricanes.

Millions of monarchs arrive in Mexico and cling to lofty fir trees in the mountains. They roost there until early March, then they head north to search for milkweed plants to feed their young. By summer, their offspring will be living as far north as Canada. These butterflies will return to Mexico in the fall. They will know how to get there without anybody showing them the way!

Brush-footed Butterflies

FAMILY: Nymphalidae
COMMON EXAMPLE: Buckeye butterfly
GENUS AND SPECIES: *Junonia coenia*
WINGSPAN: 2 to 2 1/2 inches (50 to 63 mm)

The buckeye is a dark brown butterfly with large bright spots on its wings that look like eyes. The eyespots are black with blue centers and yellow rims. If a buckeye sees an enemy, it shakes its wings. Then the eyespots look as if they are blinking. The blinking eyespots scare young inexperienced birds, but older birds are not fooled so easily.

Buckeyes also fly fast and zigzag often. This makes them hard to catch. While they sip flower juices, the butterflies are always watching for enemies. When a male is not feeding, he looks for dirt roads or other patches of bare dirt and waits for a female to come by. If it is cool weather, the male spreads his wings wide. He basks in the sun's rays to warm up his body. If it is hot, the male brings his wings together over his back and cools down.

When a male buckeye spots a female, he flies near her in a special way. First he hovers, then he gently flutters. If she likes him, they will mate. Then she flies off to lay her eggs on several kinds of plants.

When cold weather comes, many adult buckeyes migrate south to places that have mild winters. Other buckeyes creep under loose bark or into a woodpile. They stay there until the days grow warmer.

Tiger Moths

FAMILY: Arctiidae

COMMON EXAMPLE: Isabella tiger moth

GENUS AND SPECIES: *Pyrrharctia isabella*

WINGSPAN: 1 3/4 to 2 1/4 inches (44 to 57 mm)

Most people have seen a woolly bear caterpillar, but few people know that it becomes an Isabella tiger moth when it turns into an adult. The wings of the male adult are light orange-brown with one dark spot in the center of each forewing. The orange-brown female Isabella tiger moth is larger than the male. Her wings have faint brown lines and small black spots near the edges, and her hind wings have a lot of pink in them. Her well-rounded body is also orange with dark spots. The caterpillar looks very different.

A woolly bear caterpillar is born from an egg in spring. Like all caterpillars, it immediately starts to eat. It rarely stops. As it grows larger, the caterpillar molts its exoskeleton again and again. Like other caterpillars, the woolly bear's pudgy body is divided into parts called segments. Each segment has a row of black, brown, or orange fur or bristles on it. You can easily count the rows. At each molt, there is less black fur and more brown fur. The oldest caterpillars have the most brown fur. A woolly bear's thick fur protects it from birds. The fur tastes bad, so birds don't like to eat it.

In fall, a woolly bear looks for a safe place to curl up and hide for a deep winter's sleep. When warm weather wakes it up again, the caterpillar weaves its furry coat into a cozy cocoon and turns into a moth. The adult sleeps all day, but at night it flutters forth in search of a mate.

Sphinx Moths

FAMILY: Sphingiidae
COMMON EXAMPLE: White-lined sphinx moth
GENUS AND SPECIES: *Hiles lineata*
WINGSPAN: 2 3/4 to 3 1/4 inches (69 to 82 mm)

A white-lined sphinx moth darts from flower to flower as its fast wings hum. First it hovers in front of one flower, and then it whizzes away to another. It sounds just like a hummingbird! But it is a moth, and it searches for flower juices in the late afternoon or early evening. The sphinx moth sips them through its long strawlike tongue that reaches deep into a flower.

When this moth is a caterpillar, it has a smooth, dark green or black skin with yellow stripes. Its body has many segments, and there is a pointed horn on its rear end. The horn does not sting and has no poison. Sometimes the caterpillar rears up and wags its head back and forth to scare its enemies.

The caterpillar drops *frass* from the rear end of its body. Frass is made of parts of leaves that the larva cannot digest, and it is ball-shaped and greenish black. If you see frass, it means a caterpillar is nearby. The caterpillar eats and grows fat. Then it digs its way into the ground and shapes a little cave where it changes into an adult. A sphinx moth pupa looks like a little bottle with handles. After a time, the pupa wiggles out of the soil. Out creeps a damp moth, which soon dries its wings and flies off into the night.

22

Brush-footed Butterflies

FAMILY: Nymphalidae
COMMON EXAMPLE: Great spangled fritillary
GENUS AND SPECIES: *Speyeria cybele*
WINGSPAN: 3 1/2 to 3 3/4 inches (88 to 95 mm)

The great spangled fritillary has tawny orange or brown upper wings spotted with ovals, crescents, and lines of black. The underwings are light orange, spotted with black and silver patches. On the upper wings near the body, it looks as if someone has applied a little black spray paint.

The females mate in June or July, but they hide out until late August or September. Then they come out of hiding, ready to lay eggs. They lay them near violets, but not always right *on* the violet plants.

The newly hatched larvae must creep about until they find their food plant. They blend in well with their surroundings. They have black bodies decked out

24

with orange and black spines. Even after caterpillars find some violets, they do not start eating right away. Instead, they curl up on the violet plants and rest until the next spring. But when spring comes, they are terribly hungry! They start eating and they eat all night. They even munch on violets in the dark.

Brush-footed Butterflies

FAMILY: Nymphalidae
COMMON EXAMPLE: Question mark butterfly
GENUS AND SPECIES: *Polygonia interrogationis*
WINGSPAN: 2 3/8 to 2 5/8 inches (60 to 66 mm)

Question mark butterflies have wings that look jagged. This butterfly's scientific name means "many angles." In summer, their wings are dark orange with dark brown markings. But in spring and fall, their hind wings and tails develop a bright violet border. Once these butterflies were called violet tips. Then someone noticed that each hind wing has a mark like a little silver comma. Near each comma is a tiny silver dot. Together, these marks look like question marks. Violet tips gained a new name.

Some northern question marks go south when the weather becomes too cool for them. They fly in huge groups along the edge of the sea until they reach a place that is warmer. But not all of them migrate. Some of them spend the winter in protected places, such as under bark or beneath a fallen tree. When spring comes, they creep out of their hiding places and look for food. Some drink sap from leaky places on twigs. They like sap from birch, elm, willow, and maple trees.

Question marks like the juice of rotting fruit. Sometimes they become so full of fruit juice that they flip right over and go to sleep on their backs in the hot sun. For a while, they are too dizzy and sleepy to move. Question marks also sip minerals from animal droppings and mud puddles. Sometimes these butterflies will sip salty sweat from humans! When they have sipped up enough minerals, they look for flower juices.

Gossamer-winged Butterflies

FAMILY: Lycaenidae
COMMON EXAMPLE: Gray hairstreak
GENUS AND SPECIES: *Strymon melinus*
WINGSPAN: 1 to 1 1/4 inches (25 to 32 mm)

The gray hairstreak has wings that are brown on the top and light gray underneath. Its head sports black-and-white banded antennae. Can you guess how the hairstreak got its name? Take a look at its hind wings. They have bright orange spots and hairlike tails. When the swiftly moving butterfly streaks from flower to flower, its tiny hairlike tails trail behind it.

When a gray hairstreak perches, it stands with its head pointed down. The ends of the wings with orange eyespots point up. The orange spots look like eyes, and the thin hairlike tails look like antennae. A hungry bird may be fooled. It grabs the butterfly by what looks like its head, but it only gets a mouthful of wings!

In the afternoon, while female gray hairstreaks flutter around fields, males perch on small trees and shrubs. They are waiting for females to fly by. Whenever the males see a butterfly sailing by on the breeze, they dart out to look it over. If it is a female hairstreak, they become excited and flutter around trying to attract her. If she is a butterfly of another species, they fly back to their perches.

Brush-footed Butterflies

FAMILY: Nymphalidae
COMMON EXAMPLE: American painted lady
GENUS AND SPECIES: *Vanessa virginiensis*
WINGSPAN: 2 to 2 7/8 inches (50 to 72 mm)

An American painted lady's wings are speckled with orange, black, blue, and white. These colorful spots and dabs form patterns that are easy to identify. Painted ladies live in the Americas, Africa, Europe, and Asia. Some people call this insect the thistle butterfly or the cosmopolite.

Although painted ladies prefer the flower juices from thistles, they also sip from many other flowering plants. After the males feed in the afternoon, they perch on small shrubs or on the bare dirt and wait to court females.

A female lays her eggs on the top of the thistle plant, and the hatching caterpillars make a messy silk nest around the thistle leaves. They live and eat in the tent. When the larva is 1 1/4 inches long (32 mm), it changes into an adult. A butterfly emerges in about 2 weeks.

In early spring, after they have laid eggs, American painted lady butterflies migrate from the Southwest toward the North. By summer, they are everywhere in North America except the Arctic Circle. Sometimes huge groups of painted ladies migrate from Mexico.

Because neither the adults nor the larvae can survive the winter in the North, they die as the weather turns cold. New painted ladies must come from the South every spring.

Brush-footed Butterflies

FAMILY: Nymphalidae
COMMON EXAMPLE: Mourning cloak butterfly
GENUS AND SPECIES: *Nymphalis antiopa*
WINGSPAN: 2 7/8 to 3 3/8 (72 to 85 mm)

Mourning cloak butterflies live in many places—Europe, Asia, and North America. The English call them "Camberwell Beauties." Their upper wings are deep maroon with yellow borders and rows of bright blue spots. The dark, striped underside of a mourning cloak's wings matches the bark of many trees. When perched on a tree trunk, it blends in with its surroundings.

Mourning cloaks do not like woods that are too shady and cool. They live near paths, streams, sunny glades, and open places among the trees. They lay their eggs around the twigs of willows, hackberries, and elms. The newly hatched baby caterpillars move together as a group to feed. They eat almost continuously and grow rapidly.

On cool days in fall, some mourning cloaks gather in large groups and migrate to warmer climates. Other mourning cloaks crawl into cracks and crannies in woodpiles and under fallen trees. Before leaving these hideouts in spring, the butterflies warm themselves by shivering. Their wings clack together, and soon their bodies are warm enough to fly. They must be warm before they creep out, or birds can catch them easily. Sometimes a bird *does* catch one and tosses it into

the air. The mourning cloak plays dead and falls to the ground like a chip of wood. The bird takes one look and flies away. It wanted a tasty living butterfly, not a dead one.

Emperor Moths
FAMILY: Saturniidae
COMMON EXAMPLE: Polyphemus moth
GENUS AND SPECIES: *Antheraea polyphemus*
WINGSPAN: 4 to 6 inches (101 to 150 mm)

You can find polyphemus moths across the United States and in parts of Canada and Mexico. Their wing color differs, varying from a light creamy tan to reddish brown. The forewings each have a light spot on them, and the hind wings appear to have eyes.

Each hind wing has a large gray spot with a lemon yellow eye shape near the lower border of the gray. The yellow eye surrounds a transparent center, or eyespot. The moth was named after the one-eyed giant Cyclops in *The Odyssey*, by Homer. When the moth shows the eyespots on its wings, it appears to have glaring eyes.

In the North, the pupa spends the winter in a snug silk cocoon—sometimes wrapped in leaves or grass. In spring, it dissolves some of the sticky substance binding the silk strands. It uses sharp points, called beaks, on its forewing to cut open a hole. Then, noisily rocking and rolling, it uses its strong legs to push its body out through the hole.

The bright green polyphemus moth caterpillar is very hungry when it comes out. It eats and grows until it is about 4 inches (101 mm) long. Its fat, green, accordian-like body and hairy red spots help it to blend in with its surroundings. Just try to find it among the green leaves it loves to eat!

Emperor Moths

FAMILY: Saturniidae
COMMON EXAMPLE: Luna moth
GENUS AND SPECIES: *Actias luna*
WINGSPAN: 3 to 4 1/2 inches (75 to 113 mm)

The luna moth is never hungry! As a caterpillar, it ate enough to last the moth's whole lifetime. The luna moth also has no working mouthparts, so it can't eat. It spends its time looking for a mate and laying eggs. Out of the eggs come tiny caterpillars. They find themselves high in the branches of a walnut, birch, sweet gum, or hickory tree.

Luna caterpillars eat their way from leaf to leaf without stopping. Their green bodies become long and stout. They grow small lumps, bumps, and hairs on every segment. After they have molted several times, they become big enough to spin cocoons and change into adults. They roll up in leaves, shape them around their bodies, and tie them in place with silk threads. Soon they are hidden from sight.

Later, the luna moth comes out. It has beautiful light green wings with reddish edges. All four wings have eyespots. Two of them are almost as clear as tiny windows. The hind wings have long curved tails. When the luna moth sleeps on a twig, its tails lie side by side. They look like stems, and the wings look like leaves. This insect is well hidden from its enemies.

Emperor Moths

FAMILY: *Saturniidae*
COMMON EXAMPLE: Cecropia moth
GENUS AND SPECIES: *Hyalophora cecropia*
WINGSPAN: 4 1/2 to 6 inches (113 to 150 mm)

The cecropia moth belongs to the giant silkmoth family. Its large wings have beautiful patterns in white, brown, orange, and pink. The forewings have black spots on them that look like little eyes. The female moth has two tiny, red spots on the tips of her forewings and two silver spots. She has a red-and-tan striped, furry body.

The female cecropia lays from 200 to 300 eggs on the leaves of many kinds of hardwood trees. Sometimes she chooses fruit trees in orchards. When a hungry caterpillar hatches, it eats a lot and grows quickly. The stiff exoskeleton on the outside of its soft body is soon too tight. The caterpillar must molt, and a new larger skin puffs out and hardens.

Each time a caterpillar molts, its skin is a new color—black, then yellow, then green. The bumps on its skin, called *tubercles*, become blue and orange. Surprisingly, these colors help it hide among the leaves. In 4 to 6 weeks, it will be 3 to 4 inches (80 to 100 mm) long and fat.

As the weather grows cold, the caterpillar weaves a sturdy brown, silk cocoon in which it molts for the last time. Then it becomes a pupa. In spring, the pupa splits open and a wrinkled, damp moth

creeps out. It pumps fluid into its wings until they are full size. Then it drains out the fluid and lets its wings dry. Off it flies to look for a mate.

Tent Builders

FAMILY: Lasiocampidae
COMMON EXAMPLE: Eastern tent caterpillar
  moth
GENUS AND SPECIES: *Malacosoma americanum*
WINGSPAN: 1 1/2 to 2 inches (38 to 50 mm)

Plump-bodied Eastern tent caterpillar moths have two white stripes on each fringed, brown forewing. The moths lay their black egg masses on cherry, apple, or oak trees. They know just which leaves their offspring like to eat. The egg masses look like blackened marshmallows on a stick. The eggs hatch in spring, and the caterpillars spin small tents out of silk. Then out they go to eat leaves.

The caterpillars soon have plump, dark gray bodies with blue and reddish-brown markings. They leave their tents each morning and return later to rest. Because they eat continuously, their tents soon get soiled by frass. Then the caterpillars spin a new, bigger layer of silk around the outside of the old tents. They move into the clean layer and leave the old layer behind. The tents become bigger.

Every day, the caterpillars go further away from the nest to eat. If they eat all the leaves on one tree, they must search for another tree. When they are large enough to make cocoons, the caterpillars often travel far from their nests. You may find their cocoons in woodpiles, on houses, and on tree trunks.

Looking for Moths and Butterflies

Moths are active at night.

Most moths rest during the day and fly about at night as they eat, find mates, and lay eggs. Although they are hard to see in the dark, they are attracted to street lights and porch lights. Those are good places to find them.

Here is a recipe for bait to attract moths. It works best in spring or early fall when there are not too many flowers blooming. Make a mixture of sugar, ripe bananas or peaches, and a little honey. Paint this mixture on a tree. Moths smell tasty, sweet things from very far away. They will fly to the sugared tree and eat. At night, shine a flashlight on the tree you painted. You may see some wonderful species of moths eating the bait.

If you hold a butterfly, you may harm it.

Moths flutter quietly through the dark skies at night, but butterflies prefer a sunny day. When a butterfly flits from flower to flower, it looks as if it would be easy to catch. But just try! It can see you coming, and it dodges and darts this way and that. Each time you try to grab it, it zigzags away and you catch only empty air. How lucky for the butterfly that it's so quick! Human hands have oils on them that injure a butterfly's wings. Even the gentlest person's hands are likely to rub off some scales or break a little piece of wing. Even when you use a butterfly net carefully, you may hurt the butterfly.

It is better to become a butterfly conservationist. Look at butterflies with your eyes or through binoculars. Or plant flowers to attract them. Some of the many flowers that butterflies like to feed on are aster, butterfly bush, goldenrod, impatiens, lavender, lupine, marigolds, purple coneflowers, snapdragons, and zinnias. You can have a small patio or a large yard and still enjoy watching moths and butterflies.

Words to Know

antenna (plural, **antennae**)—a long projection on the head of some animals that is used to sense the world around them

chrysalis—the somewhat stiff case surrounding the pupa of butterflies

class—a group of creatures within a phylum that shares certain characteristics

cocoon—a soft spun or woven case surrounding and protecting the pupa of a moth

exoskeleton—the hard outer shell of insects and other arthropods

family—a group of creatures within an order that shares certain characteristics

frass—the solid waste or droppings of a caterpillar

genus (plural **genera**)—a group of creatures within a family that shares certain characteristics

habitat—the environment where a plant or animal lives, grows, and has young

insect—a small animal with a three-part body, six legs, and a hard outer shell called an exoskeleton

kingdom—one of the five divisions into which all living things are placed: the animal kingdom, the plant kingdom, the fungus kingdom, the moneran kingdom, and the protist kingdom

larva (plural **larvae**)—a newly hatched wormlike creature that will eventually become a moth or butterfly through metamorphosis

metamorphosis—the process of change from one form to another

migrate—to travel from one place to another to find food or to have young

molt—to shed and regrow an exoskeleton. Most insects and other arthropods molt several times before becoming adults.

order—a group of creatures within a class that shares certain characteristics

phylum (plural **phyla**)—a group of creatures within a kingdom that shares certain characteristics

pupa—the third stage of insect metamorphosis, usually a resting stage, when the larvae turn into adults

scales—the millions of extremely tiny, colored shinglelike particles on a lepidopteran's wing

species—a group of animals within a genus that shares certain characteristics. Members of a species can mate and produce young.

tubercles—tiny bumps on the exoskeleton of some caterpillars

Learning More

Books

Bailey, Donna. *Butterflies*. Chatham, NJ: Raintree/Steck-Vaughn, 1995.

Hamilton, Kersten R. *The Butterfly Book: A Kid's Guide to Attracting, Raising, and Keeping Butterflies*. Santa Fe, NM: John Muir, 1997.

Norsgaard, E. Jaediker. *Butterflies for Kids*. Minocqua, WI: Northword Press, 1996.

Pascoe, Elaine. *Butterflies and Moths*. Woodbridge, CT: Blackbirch Press, 1997.

Pringle, Laurence. *An Extraordinary Life: The Story of a Monarch Butterfly*. New York: Orchard Books, 1997.

Videos

Butterfly & Moth. Dorling Kindersley Vision.
Butterfly World: Jewels of the Sky. DaVal Productions.

Web Sites

Butterflies of North America
http://www.npsc.nbs.gov/resource/distr/lepid/bflyusa/bflyusa.htm

Moths of North America
http://www.npwrc.usgs.gov/resource/distr/lepid/moths/mothsusa.htm
The Northern Prairie Wildlife Center maintains these excellent sites. Both offer a wealth of information on species and feature photographs, checklists, and distribution maps.

Index

About the Author

Dr. **Ilka List** is an artist, author, environmental educator, and adjunct professor at State University of New York at New Paltz. For eight years as a naturalist and educator at the Mohonk Preserve, she guided children and adults onto the preserve's 6,000 semi-wild acres (2,428 hectares) to play, explore, and learn about nature. In 1998, she completed her doctoral research on "The Impact of Experience in Nature on Children's Drawings."

Dr. List has written four other children's books about nature: *A Walk in the Forest*, *Questions and Answers about Seashore Life*, *Grandma's Beach Surprise*, and *Let's Explore the Shore*. She loves to roam and ramble in wild places. She likes to teach people of all ages to love these places too.